EN AZTLÁN

WPR BOOKS: LATINO INSIGHTS
CARLSBAD, CA

WPR BOOKS: Latino Insights

3445 Catalina Dr., Carlsbad, CA 92010-2856

www.WPRbooks.com   760-434-1223   kirk@whisler.com

©2014 by MEChA de Palomar
Printed in the United States of America. All Rights Reserved.
ISBN 978-1889379-33-3

While every precaution has been taken in the preparation of this book, the author and publisher assume no responsibility for errors or omissions, or for damages resulting from the use of the information contained herein.

For more about books presented by WPR Publishing, please go to:
WWW.WPRBOOKS.COM

EN AZTLÁN

EDITORIAL TEAM

MANAGING EDITOR
John Eduardo Valdez

ASSOCIATE EDITOR
Linda Rockafellow Michlein

ASSISTANT EDITORS
Lorena Duarte
Jennifer Ferrer
Litza Ferrer
Sherrie Gonzales-Kolb
Sara Jacobsen
Claudia Marroquin
Lisette Medina
Ricardo Mendoza

EN AZTLÁN is a book of letters and arts published by Palomar College MEChA. It was published and edited by the *En Aztlán* editorial staff at Palomar College. Business correspondence, including that related to subscriptions and advertising, should be directed to: John Valdez, *En Aztlán*, Palomar College, San Marcos, CA 92069-1487.

Unsolicited manuscripts will be considered for future issues and submission deadlines are on the MEChA website (**www.facebook.com/mechadepalomarcollege**). Though we will exercise all due care in handling manuscripts, we are not responsible for loss; please keep copies of submitted work. The freedom to opinions, views, and modes of expression in this periodical is supported by *En Aztlán*. The views expressed herein, however, are those of the authors, not the editors or sponsors.

©2014 by *En Aztlán*. Authors of individual works retain copyright, with the restriction that subsequent publication of any text be accompanied by a notice of prior publication in *En Aztlán*.

Call for Submissions

En Aztlán will accept poems, fiction, non-fiction, drawings, and photography for review for our next publication. Submit work by the deadline found on the MEChA website (**www.facebook.com/mechadepalomarcollege**) to John Valdez, Managing Editor, *En Aztlán*, Palomar College, San Marcos, 92069-1487.

Keep in Touch

Visit the MEChA Alumni and Friends de Palomar College facebook page:
https://www.facebook.com/pages/MEChA-Alumni-and-Friends-de-Palomar-College/395373627220707

We have also created a MEChA Alumni and Friends de Palomar College Membership Form:
https://docs.google.com/spreadsheet/viewform?formkey=dEduZk1HT2FMLWVrUjBYYklKM1BYTFE6MQ#gid=0

Dedication

It is through the oral history of our ancestors that we can find that sense of belonging to something more than ourselves. It cannot be denied that the blood of our ancestors runs through our veins. It is through the telling of their lives that we ground ourselves in our own personal journeys.

~ Linda Amador

This collection is dedicated to our student leaders and supporters who work, study and struggle for social justice, and to Palomar College MEChA members past, present and future, as well as their service and dedication to *La Causa*.

Thank you to all who have contributed and assisted Diana Ortiz in this literary and artistic project. In appreciation to Dale Wallenius and Palomar College Foundation for their contribution in funding the mural art project in Room SU-17, the former MEChA office. Thank you to all of the artists, Joey Azul, Ruben Ochoa, Pablo Rojero Olquin, Jesus Sanchez and Adrian Donnis, for creating the MEChA mural entitled *¡Adelante MEChA Adelante!*

Thanks to Diana Ortiz, President of MEChA who facilitated and led (2000) the movement to bring about the mural project for MEChA in the former MEChA office in Room SU-17 at Palomar College.

Special thanks to Professors Doug Durant, Harry Bliss, Dean Gene Jackson, Jose Rangel, and Dr. Luz Garzon for their unfailing support and dedication.

IN LOVING MEMORY OF MARIA CONSUELO ALCALA
(1951 – 1998)

TABLE OF CONTENTS

Hear their Voices
An introduction

Dreams, hopes, and struggles flower in the barrio and
el Corazón de Aztlán to create moments of hope, love, and
joy, as well as, times of sacrifice, disappointment and pain.
Hear their voices. See their images of tenderness, which reveal
love, power, light, mystery, and sorrow. Now a new generation
is emerging among us, seeking the sun and sky in search of
oneness. With great pride we will listen and observe the voices
and photos, and honor the artists and writers who find a way to
create and communicate their souls through their art.

We desire that you enjoy our first publication of *En Aztlán*
and that you will support our efforts to do more to empower
our inspired artists, writers and student leaders in MEChA
who are dedicated to community service. With great
enthusiasm we introduce to you the very talented artists,
writers, and leaders—*en Aztlán.*

John Eduardo Valdez
Professor of Multicultural Studies and
MEChA Advisor, Palomar College

Sin Título
Ricardo Mendoza

te
detiene
espléndido
tirastre
de segunda
llamada
releva
tu
termino
deseo
la voz
enterrada
y aunque
tu son
sonante
del alma
arrojaste,
el silencio
es la tumba
que nos
envuelve.

To You...

Sherrie Gonzales-Kolb

Let us speak of this, you who are wisest, even if it be bad.
Silence is worse, all truths that are kept silent become poisonous.

~ Nietzsche, *Thus Spoke Zarathustra*

If it had not been in the best interest of everyone,
I would not have remained silent—in the harmless intensity
of my passive passion for you.
I am a poet…words the medium by which I purge…
Silence is torturous for logophiles…
The Universe and its contents touch us, regenerate us,
perpetually hurling us into daily metamorphoses…toward
Nirvana, Immortality…Completion…
Who can remain Silent under the constant Spell of Life?
Then the gnawing away for Expression…
The compulsion to speak Truth…
No matter who is undone by the fires that burn inside
us…building toward Spontaneous Combustion…
like a geyser restrained too long by human
intervention….setting itself free….
And then Jesus said, "It is finished."

Hubiera Querido Ser Espíritu
Ricardo Mendoza

Un espíritu yo hubiera querido ser
como el sol, como el agua
haber nacido sin cuerpo
sin ti y sin yo
labrando espumas en los ríos
sudando arco irises en los vientos
marcando besos en tus labios
Un espíritu hubiera querido ser yo
para jugar con los voces y sonidos detonaes
entonados en los tonos del otoño
sobre primavera en la nieve
cascabeles perfumadas de gusanos de seda
telaraña negra espeja que refleja el sal de tu sudar
Hubiera querido ser espíritu sin sangre en las montañas
cuchillos de obsidiana sembrando rayos de luz
en la pisca de desiertos
pudiese haber sido maguey
sin espinas y sin pie o carne
Hubiera querido ser espíritu
en vez de ser lágrimas de espíritus
que llaman en silencio al pensamiento del ceniciento
de gentes torturadas

Hubiera querido ser espíritu
no más ni menos, manito, manita
la olla de suero del mundo mandano común popular,
vulgar
el macho domina la hembra
sin tierra mejor coje cemento quebrado en arena
cincuenta devuelta al cien-fuegos, o al siete leguas
leyendas tomadas de pisco sereno
cocaína en plantas de elote
la hoja sagrada de cristo en espinas
con clavos de tétano
mosos enmoesidos
del poco dinero al niño sereno
muerto en gusanos
no de seda sino de la miseria
corriendo a la tienda
hacerle los mandados a los ricos cobardes
chanates, cuervos y gatos negros
de la bruja blanca dominando al don juan
el yaqui o yanke go home
con libros alienantes como jirafas rojas de sangre
llorona sin pueblo quemando bajo bombas, bombinas
de niñas sin dientes
Hubiera querido ser espíritu mayor en vez de lo que soy.

Genesis: A Roadtrip Through the Formative Years
Sherrie Gonzales-Kolb

When I was eight years old, the highway was my pathway to the other side of the Universe, to a place my parents longingly called home. My home was California; their home was in the faraway land called Texas—the other side of my eight-year-old world— and to a place which I would later understand to be—the other side of myself.

The first summer I journeyed to my parent's homeland was met with anxiety and trepidation; I had never been outside of my small world of California, and I had heard all of the stories that comprised my parents' lives, lives that were constructed "back home" in their turbulent beginning, and so, my beginning as well.

I knew that my grandfather Lon was the "meanest son-of-a-bitch" who ever lived, "even tougher than John Wayne," who continued to be my father's patron saint until his death. And my Grandma Lupe was also purported to be somewhat of a "saint" although in every picture that I had ever seen of her, she looked meaner than the grandfather who I had heard about all my life.

Then there was my cousin Paz who was old, but who had never married. He still lived with his mom, my Tía Chona. Paz was a "mama's boy" and perhaps, even "*un maricón*," but he was my cousin, my second cousin, which made him as old as my father, and I was to treat him with the respect that was given to elders.

"Daddy, what's a *maricón*?" I remember asking that morning we left for Texas.

My father laughed very hard and said, "Uh, go ask your mother."

"Mom, what's a *maricón*?"

"Sherrie Ann, that's an ugly word! Now, hurry up and go pee, we have a long drive ahead of us. Macedonio, I don't know why you tell the kids such ugly things!"

On our three day trip "back home" we would hear so many more variations of the stories about the places we would visit and the people we would meet—stories that my mother told us were full of "skeletons" in the history of our "people."

"Well, your mother's people are all fat—but you kids take after my people. Thanks to God!" offered my father.

"Hell, at least my people aren't a bunch of goddamned drunks!" My mother would respond angrily, and then equally as reflexive and penitent, "Ay, God forgive me!"

My father would laugh because he was, as my mother often told us, such a "goddamned tease," and my mother would sulk from Fallbrook to Yuma, Arizona.

Genesis: A Roadtrip (cont.)

As we would arrive at our first area for the night, I remember
hearing an unfamiliar whirring in the Arizona trees.
The darkness of night would surround me in a strangeness
of a place that was not my home, or my parents' home.

"Daddy, is that noise *La Llorona*?" I would ask, terrified to hear
his answer.

"Yes," he would reply, "now let's go and see if we can find her."

La Llorona was a witch who lived in trees and who would
take children's souls, and the only way to kill her was to recite
the Apostle's Creed backwards.

"Daddy, do you know the Apostle's Creed backwards?" I asked,
not quite certain that my father really knew everything.

"Yes," he would offer with the poker face his gambling father had
taught him, "now, let's go."

"Let me hear you say it then," a brave request because my father's
wrath was much more immediate than *La Llorona*'s.

"Don't be such a big baby. I'm just playing with you—besides
La Llorona lives only in Texas and I have connections there.
I know a witch named Doña Pancha and she knows the Apostle's
Creed backwards—and, besides, she can mix us up a potion
so that *La Llorona* won't even come near us while we're there.
As a matter of fact, Doña Pancha is the only woman in the
history of Lampasas who has ever seen *La Llorona* and she
recited the Apostle's Creed backwards and when she finished,

La Llorona fell dead, straight to the ground!"

With my eyes as big as the lie he had just told, "Really?! Then she's dead, Daddy, and she can't hurt us!"

"*No, hombre!* She comes back to life as soon as you leave her presence. You have to recite the prayer every time you run across her."

I knew then that I didn't want to go to this place called Texas and if I had known how to survive in this great big Universe without my parents, I would have run all the way back home to the safety of my Fallbrook and its beautiful trees, where *La Llorona* would never be.

"Macedonio, quit scaring her! Sherrie Ann, let's go wash up for the night. It's okay, *m'hija*, those are just stories from your father's superstitious people—they are not true. Baptists don't believe in that nonsense. Your father's people are Catholic. They have all sorts of silly stories!"

"Yes, they are too true, Stella! I saw *La Llorona* myself when I was just a boy and I just barely escaped her!"

I ran to my mother's side at Light Speed—away from my father and his scary stories—confused that he would want to go back to such a place where witches lived in trees. I would toss and turn all night asking God to keep us safe from *La Llorona*—and wishing that I had paid attention better in catechism so that I could have known the Apostle's Creed forward and would have had something to work from should I have found myself face-to-face with this evil thing named *La Llorona*. (To be continued…)

Medicine Woman MICA VALDEZ

Old Scraps of Paper: A Collage

Sherrie Gonzales-Kolb

Tight-fisted metaphors
refusing to bloom…clenched in suspense—
will not,
must not,
can not.
There is no safety in numbers. A clandestine solo affair.
A secret conception.
An intentionally unanswered question. A spot on white linen.
An ugly Truth revealed.
The stroke of midnight—an inconsequential moment in
the history of humanity.
A god who has been silenced in the marketplace of relic
deities, sold at roadside stands and flea markets for pocket
change, no more than a trinket on the dash of the phallic
automobile. The license plate on a powder-blue Jag that
reads, "godsblsng."
An unfinished poem. A closet recluse.
A disavowal of instincts, obligatory in an ordered world—
achieved through the domestication of animals...
"then he paired them in twos, a male with his female…where
there will be weeping and gnashing of teeth…"

OLD SCRAPS OF PAPER (CONT.)

The birth pangs of civilization—(no pain, no gain).
Repression, the loincloth of humankind—a global
delusion…
An unsanctioned consummation of primeval urges, but
Holy, nonetheless.
The birth of a nation…the death of a species.
Uncharted territory…
infancy, puberty, maturing to a ripe old age, yet infinitely,
to know, to know, to know
that "…with great wisdom [also] comes great pain."
Creation in a dew drop.
The Cosmos in a reluctant tear.
Running away then coming back.
To love then hate then to love again.
Lost in the intensity of illusory emotions—
then still and rational.
Unsteady legs on perfectly balanced ground (but the mind
is lucid).
"…the Spirit is willing but the flesh is weak."
A zygotic thought never to breathe the Breath of Life—
choked by the umbilicus of ego:
Culture, a quick, albeit temporary fix, necessary because
"…they do not know the difference between their right and
left hands…"
(still don't)
Would the Good Shepherd not leave the ninety-nine to
recover the once lost lamb? An ancient tale? or was it a
nursery rhyme? Like the old lady in the shoe who was
supposed to teach young girls about Contraception—or
was it something altogether different?

An old wives' tale?
Nothing makes sense and sometimes life is too long.
Innocence, now and oh-so-distant memory; and
disenchantment brings no diversion.
Perception is big clumps of clay in tiny, clumsy hands.
No fusion of complete comprehension—a variegated
version of "almost but not quites" and
strong, like a mutt.

Aristotle's "approximation of the Truth…"
Not whose, not wha—
a singularity in form—
Expressionless.
Surely there is an infinitesimal trace of Cohesion in all of this chaos.
A single mustard seed in Nineveh.

A chard, a shred, a Gravitational Force…

Untitled Mica Valdez

MURAL NOTES: REFLECTIONS ON THE MEChA MURAL AT PALOMAR COLLEGE

JOEY AZUL

Ruben Ochoa asked my friend Jesus Sanchez and me if we would like to work on a mural for MEChA.

Originally the intent of the mural was to focus on MEChA, its function and history. We set out to develop images and ideas which we felt would represent the Latino community at Palomar College.

We gathered references individually about the history of Hispanic people in America, recent history, and pre-Colombian. We got together about once a month for many months and sketched and shared ideas. We also talked a lot about what was important about what the mural would mean to those who view it. We shared our own stories and concerns about life.

For a while we thought to make a mural focusing on great Mexican artists, who by their work represent so much of struggle and successes of Latino people. It almost came to be that the focal figures of the mural were Frida Kahlo, (Jose Clemente) Orozco, (Diego) Rivera and (David Alfaro) Siqueiros.

MURAL NOTES (CONT.)

The plan then changed to a schemata which was more
personally (particular) representative of Palomar College itself.
To honor teachers, and by this reference the educational process
became the central theme. Four teachers were selected based
on their significant contributions.

The concept of change, transition, possibility, became a guide
in the selection of symbols and images. The day to night
sky, sun and moon, these, as well as contemporary scenes of
Palomar, in the midst of pre-Colombian reference are examples
of this concern.

It is interesting to note that we never were at a loss for
images, but had some difficulty in editing our richness of
ideas. Sometimes agreeing, and sometimes not, we each had
attachments to certain things others didn't always have.
This speaks, I think for the richness of history and experience
from which the mural concepts were taken. It mirrors also
the struggle for identity we all have in negotiating our way
in a rapidly changing world.

We always wanted a strong central focus, we chose a sun.
The sun went through several versions, finishing with a more
contemporary revision. Pablo Rojero Jr. joined the team during
the final composition detailing. Near to the sun are students.
It was a specific request by MEChA to represent students when
we could do so. A history of student involvement is expressed
by the protest marchers. We researched newspaper photos to be
accurate. Front and center, are students engaged in their studies.

Finally, we wanted to include a reference to spirit, both the traditional heritage and that represented by the presence of the Mission.

The mural became after a while, an entity on its own. We no longer were making it. It became something we had to adjust our ideas to. We learned a lot about a cooperative working process, and much about ourselves. We were running out of time at the end of summer. But we took no shortcuts. Even after the dedication we returned in off times to do detailing.

HARD TIMES

JOSÉ JAIMES

Have you ever looked up at the sky?
And set your eyes upon a star?
Thinking of that special someone.
The one who's your everything?
The one who has captured your heart and soul?
Her eyes, her smile, her hair.
Oh! If only she was yours.

Lowering your eyes,
That glowing passion towards her turns to emptiness,
Your mind going blank,
Your throat going dry,
And your heart beats fast.

Moments later,
You find yourself staring straight ahead,
Staring at nothing in particular,
As you whirl to a state of oblivion.

The night becomes cold and gloomy,
Adding to that emptiness,
Which turns to loneliness,
Feeling like a lost soul in a crowded world.

As your mind comes back to reality,
All you find yourself thinking is about her.
Thinking that if only she was yours,
The world as you know it would be different,
If only she was yours,
If only you had a chance.

You level your eyes to that same star once again and ask why?
Why is it that you seem to always fall for the impossible ones?
Thinking that it would be easier to reach for that star than her heart.
But if only you had a chance to win her heart,
You would be staring at her eyes rather than at that star.

THE DANCE
LINDA AMADOR

Time. Time eternal. Nothing really changes. The dance is danced
as it always has, only the partners change. This was brought
home to me recently when I had my parents over for dinner.
The leftovers had been removed as we three settled back in our
chairs. The hour was early and it called for another round of
fresh-brewed coffee. I sat there between these two aged-loving
human beings, wondering under what circumstances they
had met, fallen in love and married. So I asked them. And the
story of the dance, began. As the steam from the coffee traveled
upward it seemed as if the years evaporated. I was forgotten as
they stared in to the distance and began to relate the events of so
long ago. To a time which I could only glimpse as through a veil
but which they saw clearly as thought it were yesterday.

We were transported to Conutillo, Texas, 1937. As they spoke
I could almost feel the heat and dust from the dirt streets. The
streets lined with square box houses made of brown adobe. Plain
brown houses on plain brown streets against a plain brown hot
sky. The summer sun beat down on the row of flat roof tops.
Rooms sparsely furnished. Agriculture packing crates were used
as furniture. Crates for cabinets, crates for tables and crates
for chairs. Always a crucifix adorned one wall. A bed and the
necessary wooden stove to cook the slap-slapped tortillas and
refried *frijoles* completed the scene.

To look for street signs on the corners would have been fruitless because there weren't any. But there wasn't any need for street signs. Everyone knew everyone in the small *barrio*. And all the streets led to one central place. This was the daily gathering place of the young. It was here that the rituals of the dance took place. A ritual as timeless as time itself. This dance, a courting dance that was danced throughout the ages. It was the "well." Where youthful lasses were told to fetch clear drinkable water for coffee. And where fresh young men waited to strut and swagger in this beginning mating dance.

Before dusk they would gather by the dozens. The girls strolling in small groups, shyly glancing in the direction of the young men. In turn these lads pretended in their *macho*-ness not to notice. But the "dance" needed partners. And destiny had fixed its course.

Elvira Padilla was typically young. By our modern standards too young for lifelong decisions, but in this long ago era, old enough. Thirteen years old, with shoulder length, jet black hair, she was a slight little thing. She too, would join her friends at this "well." As these maidens grouped together, they would lean forward, heads almost touching, intently listening to what the other was saying. You could just about hear the whispering as they shared the latest gossip. Who "liked" whom, and what so-and-so had said. Their heads would nod in agreement that yes, whoever had done whatever had surely done the right thing. Suddenly one would notice that lateness of the hour. All would gasp for they remembered the dire warnings that their protective mothers had imparted to them. "Always come home before dark. And never, never, never be caught alone after dark with a man. Because after the sun has set a man could be filled with '*el diablo*' (the devil)

THE DANCE (CONT.)

and could kill you." So, as if on command, they would in unison, dash off toward home before the transition to darkness was completed. And all that would be left was the dust from several scurrying feet. As it settled, an effective tool was implemented to prevent night-covered passions from exploding by keeping all young girls home at night.

Fate had singled out the other dance partner. Catarino Labrado Amador wore his 19 years with dignity and pride. He too, worked the fields as everyone else in the barrio did, including Elvira's parents. If you looked through his open window at night he could be seen making his own tortillas in the evenings. And Elvira had caught his eye and captured his heart. But this proud young man couldn't figure out how to approach her. Time and again his friend, Manuel would tell him, "go ahead, there she is, talk to her, go talk to her now." But each opportunity would pass as Catarino's courage would fail him. Undoubtedly Elvira would hear about it through the grapevine. Nevertheless, wherever she went Catarino would somehow, appear. This did not go unnoticed by the eagle eye of Josephina, Elvira's mother.

Eventually one day, it happened. Jospehina cornered Catarino. She confronted him, demanding "Why everywhere Elvira is, you are there, too?" What could he say? Standing tall, with his shoulders back and his spine straight, Jospehina could see the determination in his eyes. Thus, Catarino responded with all the fervor in the universe, "Because I love her." His words hung in the air. Josephina knew she would need to scrutinize this particular young man. The dance was getting closer. It could be felt in the air. You could almost hear a faint note in the distance.

Eventually, one evening, Elvira was drawing water from
the well and feeling exasperated from Catarino's lack of action.
When would he ever do something, anything? Oscar, Catarino's
friend, came up to her. She stood there listening to him. Arms
folded, foot tapping, irritated. Would she have to listen to
another second-hand account of Catarino's interest? Enough was
enough. Clinching her fists, and speaking carefully and clearly,
she retorted, "Give Catarino a message for me, if he has anything
to say have him say it to me himself."

This dance partner was starting to lose patience. The turning
and twisting of the dance was taking too long. Days, weeks and
months of waiting is like eternity when you are 13 years old.
Then magically one evening, there before Elvira was Catarino.
He, himself in the flesh. She must have been delighted. Had he
received her message?

Can you hear the music, faintly, but hear it nonetheless there
in the distance? Ahhhh, at last he would speak. Words from
him, she waited to find out. But alas, to no avail, he instead
said, "What did you want? José told me that you needed to
speak to me." Elvira was crushed. That was it! The final straw!
After months of innuendos, sidelong glances, stated interests
via messengers, now he had the audacity to ask why she had
summoned him. There were limits to what this lass could take.
With a steel glint in her eyes, she lashed out, "If you were any
kind of '*hombre completo*,' (complete man), you wouldn't have
had to make up some kind of story about Jose summoning you.
I never want to see you again." With a stomping of her foot
that raised a small cloud of dust, she pivoted around and stalked
off in the opposite direction. That was that.

THE DANCE (CONT.)

But destiny had a different plan and I and my five sisters are living proof. As this rejected youth watched in disbelief the retreating figure of the girl he had declared to love, I could almost hear the deep sigh of despair escape from his lips. But remember time. To everything there is a season, and a purpose under heaven…

…three long months later, Elvira had acquired and dispensed with one boyfriend, Tony. Catarino had not been idle and he too, had a girlfriend named Teresa. It was Saturday and Elvira and Teresa were discussing the Mexican-American dance to take place that night. Teresa was so disappointed because she would not be able to attend. Elvira was going as her parents were active members.

Would Elvira do Teresa a favor and keep an eye on Catarino? Just let her know who he danced with? Of course, such a simple request. Would there be after all, a dancing of the dance? Had just the partners changed? No, the partners had been chosen, they simply needed to be readied. For the time was at hand. The music was still there but before the first note could be heard the partners must prepare themselves. Earlier that week, Elvira had just returned from her first shopping experience in a department store.

Her aunt had taken her to the large city of El Paso to buy a dress. No common dress would do. Clutching the generous amount of three dollars they traveled. At the store, she had painstakingly gone through numerous dresses on the rack, finally spotting the perfect one. It was yellow with horizontal black stripes, a cinched waist, peter pan collar, quarter length sleeves and a full skirt that would twirl out as she danced. She smiled, delighted at finding the ideal one. Yes, this was it.

When she returned home with her prize, Jospehina was appalled to discover that a size 18 dress for a 96 pound petite would never do. Elvira's aunt had neglected to inform her about dressing rooms and their purpose. Several hours and several neighbors later, the dress had been taken apart and put back together. A perfect fit for the perfect dance partner.

She slipped the dress over her head and felt the coolness of the fabric. The hem line fell just below her knee folding softly. The rustling of the dress as she walked gave her confidence, poise and grace. Elvira was prepared. A similar ritual was taking place at Catarino's house. These young men wore the same uniformed black pants, belted at the waist yet with a slight flare to give a wide pant leg. Black shoes and Cuban ones at that. High-heeled with a slightly pointed toe. Forty dollar shoes if you could afford them. Catarino could and he polished them until they shined. A white shirt with only one button unbuttoned at the pointed collar. And long sleeves turned not once or three times up, but twice, carefully rolled up.

The partners fitted in their attire. It was time to dance. The hall with chairs lined up against the two opposing walls, hosted an orchestra. There were two entrances to this building. And it was here where the men would stand. Gathered as if supporting one another emotionally. Tightly wedged as close to the door as possible. Could it be they sought the comfort of a quick escape? The first note had not been sounded. Elvira sat smoothing her dress, fussing with her hair completely unaware that a dashing

THE DANCE (CONT.)

young man had already spotted her. He focused his eye on
her and thought to himself "now is the time, it's now or never."
So as the first notes resounded through the hall, Catarino made
a beeline and found himself standing before Elvira.
With resolution yet gentleness he spoke politely, "*Gusta bailar
con migo?*" Would you care to dance with me? She would not
refuse and followed him to the dance floor.

This first dance lasted a lifetime. Slow and soft they danced,
without speaking. The music, the partners, and the dance
became one. The twirling and turning was only a prerequisite
of the twists and turns their lives would take as partners, friends,
companions, and lovers. Catarino holding Elvira for the first
time. Could it be that something deep inside told them that
this was to be the first of many dances? The first dance of a
life-dance? Probably not. We hurry through our days and only in
reflection pinpoint the magic moments that changed our course,
our destiny. This was their magic moment, this was their destiny,
the dance was set. Reluctantly, after the orchestra finished,
Catarino showed Elvira to her seat. Then quickly, resumed his
position by the entrance in the comfort and protection of the
other men. But as the next dance began Elvira looked up to see
Catarino again before her. Only this time, as they finished
the second dance, he asked her for the next one. He wasn't about
to take any chances of her dancing with another partner.
He wanted insurance that she would not dance with anyone else
but him.

This continued throughout the night. Always the polite inquiry, always the same agreement. They twirled and turned. They danced and danced. It seemed a lifetime. And it became one. Then it was the final dance, the Adios (goodbye) dance. But it was not adios, something had been settled. The new relationship was established yet the only words spoken were the request and the agreement. It had been decided. And not to everyone's surprise, it was only a matter of time before Elvira Padilla became Elvira Amador. End of story. No, just the beginning of theirs.

They stopped talking, my parents. We were quiet. They sat back and looked at each other across the table, across the years from long ago to the here and now. Enchantment filled the air. I realized the privilege of having been a passenger to witness all the events of that first dance. I couldn't resist asking, "Well, Mom, how did you feel at the end of the dance?" She answered, "Guilty, I had some explaining to do to Teresa, but I had had so much fun dancing the night away. And he was so polite." She smiled remembering, "How about you, Daddy, at the end of the dance, how did you feel?" He looked at me and slowly, the corners of his mouth turned up. The wrinkles framing his eyes became more pronounced as he, Catarino, turned to look straight into Elvira's eyes, and he spoke clearly, without hesitating, with confidence, "I felt great!"

All of a sudden we were all smiling. And you know, somehow I too, "felt great." I found much comfort in his words. In a world of small commitment and changing partners my parents had made a long term commitment. Now 65 years later they were still dancing.

The Last Painter on Earth
Alex Martinez

The old man sighed and wiped the sweat from his brow on his wide sleeve. He glanced up at the sun, perhaps a hand span from the horizon in the last hours of the day. He was a small, frail seeming Asian man, with a few wisps of facial hair—a long goatee, mustaches, and bushy gray eyebrows—on an otherwise bald head. The sandals on his feet were wooden and his clothes were simple and baggy. His eyes squinted against the light and turned away. He looked at the easel in front of him, then past at the slowly darkening landscape beyond. The canvas showed the traces of a skillful hand just beginning a masterpiece, with details just sketched in lightly, and thicker, deeper background hues already laid down.

The old man frowned at the barely started painting. He abruptly rubbed a hand across the canvas, ruining the work, and walked away. The easel stood silently for a moment, with its marred canvas facing the setting sun. Then it suddenly turned to sand, collapsing to the ground. The old man paid no heed. The paintbrush in his other hand dropped, and that too disolved into the earth.

The painter slowly strolled across the land, his hands linked behind his back, his head bowed in contemplation. He noticed the gravel of the desert environment around him, with various rocks and boulders sparingly scattered, rocky hills in the distance of one direction, and the smoother outline of dunes blending with the sky in another. And what a sky, he mused to himself. This is one of my favorites.

It was a clear cerulean merging overhead to a velvety indigo, the sun kissing the far edge with scarlet. As he walked, the old man began to change. He shifted even as the day shifted to night around him. A golden glow, soft but clearly visible, encased him, wrapping around him and curling through him. The painter grew taller. Hair sprouted from his head and fell to his shoulders, shining iridescently white, a mixture of all colors, and he became clean shaven. His ethnicity became unidentifiable as his skin swirled to a golden brown, his metamorphosis handsome. The painter's eyes continuously altered, green, brown, blue, then black and gray, and back again. His clothes also changed, flowing into an even simpler garb of loose white robes. The painter merely continued on his stroll through the evening, serenely observering the empty landscape stretching about him. Soon, however, the painter's eyebrows, now fine and elegantly flaring, knitted together in slight consternation. He pursed his lips and thought for a moment. He seemed to come to a decision and gestured fluidly with his right hand. Darkness and light swirled forth, heaving and rising from the dusk beside the painter. It writhed and twisted, lengthening and still growing, finally coalescing into the shape of a very, very large serpent with legs: a dragon.

The animal gleamed all over, its ebony scales slick with the the reflected light of a newly awakened moon. A mane of spines

THE LAST PAINTER ON EARTH (CONT.)

and horns covered the dragon's neck, riding up its brow and along the ridges above its blazing yellow eyes. Two large horns rose back at the base of its skull. The rest of its body wound its way back into the gloom, supported on two pairs of legs, ending at length in a long, lashing tail. The creature coiled and uncoiled quickly, every movement liquid lightning; it stretched its legs, streched its body to full length, holding it rigid, then flexing and loosening, coming at last to a relaxed position. The painter watched all of this calmly, standing with his hands laced together behind his back as the dragon's coils surrounded him.

The dragon's gaze took in the surrounding world. Its claws flexed in the gritty earth, digging deep trenches. Its piercing stare swung impressively to rest on the painter.

"Hello, serpent," the painter said with a small smile.

"Creator," the dragon rumbled back, never actually moving its mouth, but the words precisely reverberating in the night air despite a lack of vocal apparatus.

"Hmmm. Yes, creator. Well. You may use that term too hastily my old friend. But it's good to see you again," the white-clad man said.

"And you. If I may ask, why have you called me back so quickly, lord? You have something urgent to tell me which you forgot?" The dragon's voice filled the air, and the painter could feel it vibrating in his chest.

"No, actually, Mahatma, it has been some time since our last converstaion…a very long while, in fact." The painter smiled again. "How quickly you forget the existence of time, serpent."

"The like of you and I have no constant reminders, creator."

The painter began walking again. The length of the dragon straightened and fell into a slinking, smooth gait alongside the man. They moved in silence, as the last light of the sun disappeared and only a dusting of purple on the horizon gave any evidence there had ever been a fiery ball in the sky. The desert blanketed the two beings in silence, with only the dragon's slow inhale and exhale and the sound of the sand crunching underfoot disturbing it.

"You are troubled again, lord. Why do you say I use the term 'creator' hastily?" The dragon's tail reached around and rested gently on the painter's shoulder, stroking slowly. The painter ran a hand through his white locks.

"You remember our last conversation. Do you remember my creations, Mahatma? The paintings I told you of? Their chronology? 'In the beginning…' the void, heaven and earth, water and wind, man…" The painter gestured above and below, kicking at a pebble on the ground.

"Ah, yes, these I remember. I was even in the paintings at points was I not?" At the painter's nod, Mahatma continued.

"I remember the chronology. The series was unfinished, as I recall. Quite inspired, though. How fares it now, lord?"

The painter stopped walking and gazed at the moon. He drew a deep breath. "Revelations." The dragon nodded its massive

THE LAST PAINTER ON EARTH (CONT.)

head. "Unfortunately, I am the alpha and the omega, Mahatma. Everything must begin, and all must end." The painter glanced at the dragon. "Except you and I, it seems. But for this world, this is the exodus. Man is gone, the beasts are gone, the forests, the plains. It is done. Even the wind has left.

"So you see, serpent, I'm not only a creator, I'm a destroyer as well. None of my paintings last. Either I scrub them away, or they collapse upon themselves. Eyeblinks. I capture eyeblinks in glass bottles, and I cannot make them last. I fear I may despair of this soon, my friend."

"And yet…" the dragon purred monstrously. He swirled a huge talon in the sand, slowly creating a mound that rose up with each circular swoop of the claw, up and up, until the painter's easel was standing again, reformed from the dirt. Mahatma dragged his claws across the blank canvas, but instead of rips in the cloth, a vivid streak of crimson followed each claw. "And yet, creator, you still paint. You still try. I know this; you took the form of man just before you summoned me, and you were painting. Man was the only one of your creations that has ever painted as you do. You felt a connection, I think, lord. And now—" The dragon's movement was faster than sound; one moment he was at ease, his body relaxed against the ground, the next his tail had whipped around and viciously cut the easel in half. Immediately it fell in an explosion of sand, merging again with the earth. Mahatma scooped up a clawful of sand and let it cascade back to the ground between his talons.

"You are the loneliest being I have ever come across, painter. None see as you do, around, through, before and after: the consummate artist. But these creatures, these caricatures of yourself, they came very near to touching the sun, didn't they?

"Truly, lord, if there were more than ice flowing through these veins of mine, my heart would split asunder for you." The dragon met the painter's gaze with his own hooded golden one, entire worlds revolving in either, along with an unknowable sadness. The creator smiled again, showing only warmth for his sinuous companion. He reached out and gently tugged on one of the horns protruding from the large reptilian's head.

"You damnable serpent. You made a wonderful adversary, you know. The human race would never have fared as well as they did without you."

"Nonsense," the dragon snorted. The spines on his neck rose slightly, the scales ruffling along his back. "I made a few cameo appearances in your paintings, nothing more. The rest was simple name dropping, and the humans ran with it. 'Eat of this tree, and you shall know the world for what it is.' Absolutely ridiculous."

The painter sighed and ran his hands through his hair. It shimmered against the night, the stars themselves woven amidst its strands. "There is no simple solution to my problem, is there? I seek your counsel, serpent."

"Of course there is a simple solution, lord," Mahatma boomed. The painter could feel it in his chest again. "My simple mind can think of no other kind. Do not paint anymore. Do as I do: hunt.

THE LAST PAINTER ON EARTH (CONT.)

That would be a simple solution." The dragon paused. "But that is not your solution. You are not the hunter. You are the creator." Mahatma gathered his coils about himself, and bunched his legs underneath him, concentrating all of his considerable mass in front of the creator. He looked against the night, black on black, and leaned his giant head in nose-to-nose with his companion.

"The answer lies in this, lord," the dragon scooped up a clawful of sand again, and let it slip from his grasp; only this time, a warm breeze blew from the west, where the sun had died. It blew the sand between the two beings' faces, and lifted the painter's hair across his color-shifting eyes, around his head. His eyes widened, still locked on Mahatma's, then following the dust in the wind. "You are," the dragon said as the rest of the sand blew away, "the Last Painter on Earth." And with that the great serpent launched himself into the air, faster than thought, and slid away through the darkness of the sky.

The breeze picked up, whipping the painter's voluminous robes around him, his hair dancing to the wind. He raised his arms slowly, letting the wind catch the robes fully. He spun around, his head back, laughing. He stopped then, and returned thoughtful eyes to the moon, the wind still animating his hair and clothing.

"I am the Last Painter on Earth," he murmured to himself. He then reached out his hand and caressed the moon from the sky. He looked down at it, rolled it across his fingers thoughtfully. God then walked off into the night, the light of the moon in his palm, and the wind flying at his heels. The Last Painter on Earth.

TREES

YASUHIRO SAHARA

Like the trees in the wind bending with force

But remaining rooted

Is the struggle of *La Raza* faced with

Strength

SHE'S GONE
ARI CASTELLANOS

She's gone when I thought that we would last
She left me all alone and now I can't even concentrate.
I ask God where is she?
And to come pick me up
'Cause God I am so sad
It's funny how life works
All of a sudden you're happy
And now I am all alone
My emotions betrayed me
They told me she would never leave me
So she did and now I am all alone
And she's gone.

PERDÍ
MAINARDO FLORES

Perdí tu rostro en el viento
Tus caricias se las comió el sol
La luna se llevó tu voz
Y poco a poco te perdí

Las flores guardan tu color
Entre las nubes se fueron tus risas
El agua se quedó con tu sombra
Y poco a poco te perdí

SECRET LOVE
ERNESTO SANCHEZ

I saw you smile at a guy,
I don't know why I feel so down,
I saw you smile at me,
I don't know why I feel so weird…

I remember the times when you ran to me,
How you cried because you've been hurt,
I was there to comfort you,
And now I will always be there for you…

The smile from your lips
Makes my face warm.
I asked myself, "Why?"
I don't know the answer.
Someone told me to open my eyes,
To look deep inside my heart,
And then my heart whispered,
It is you that I love.

I can't tell anyone,
Because they might tell you,
I need to face my fears,
But it's hard to tell you that I am
in love with you.

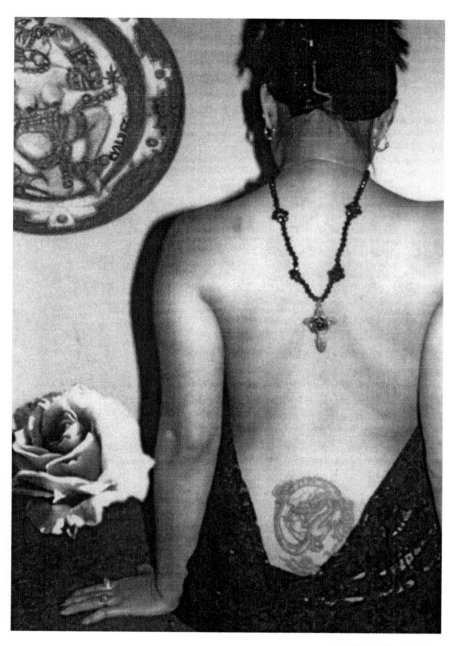

Untitled Mica Valdez

Ad Deum
John Eduardo Valdez

Oh my God, I am heartily sorry
for having offended Thee—
For Thou art all Good and deserving
of all my love
Through my fault
Through my fault
Through my most grievous fault
Mea culpa
Mea culpa
Mea maxima culpa

Introibo ad altare Dei
Ad Deum—qui letificat juventutum meam.
I will go in unto the altar of God
To God, Who giveth joy to my youth.

I go to the house of God
I go to the house of God
with beer breath,
with the breath of beer
chugged down
from a day in the sun.

I go to the house of God
with my blood stains
on Highway 80—
After my cry and the terrifying sounds

of Billy's '52 Chevy propelled
into space
and onto the sacred earth of Mission Valley—
On the day of New Year's Eve,
1955.

Billy's Chevy was beautiful,
grey-colored and lowered,
with whitewall tires
and bright-red-colored hubs—
The silver-chromed dash bars
spun before my eyes
in an instant,
As it then flew into the air
(at 70 miles an hour).
The following day, Billy,
18 years old,
Died.

I am sailing majestically upward
through clouds and sky,
Leaving the mother planet,
Leaving this mystery,
after 14 years.
Leaving my childhood memories
of Lemon Grove—
The yellow concrete Lemon
in Lemon Grove.
Leaving my childhood memories
of my Mexicanness
and confusion,

AD DEUM (CONT.)

Leaving my *colonia* on the other side
of the railroad tracks
and packing house
Leaving my life of schools
where I am lost and silent.
Leaving my *familia*,
Our Lady of Guadalupe,
and my questions of Why?
and Who I am?

I am a free spirit.
I am spirit ascending.
My Guardian Angel enfolds me.
I am at peace until—
terrified voices of earth
break the silence,
And awaken me back to the earth.

I find I am under the car—

I feel the weight of the twisted steel—

In a fraction of time, then,

The burden is lifted—

I am free—

I am in pain, but—

I am free!

Where am I?

Where am I going?

Who am I?

These questions to be continued
till a later moment of time,
To be continued on days of solitude,
Where I will roam the hills
of Lemon Grove
On my days of escape from high school.

I now return to my destined path
that takes me back where

I wonder—
I feel   I hurt
I play   I pray
          I seek
          I love
          I hope

I will go to the house of God.

Introibo ad altare Dei

Ad Deum—qui letificat juventutem meam.

I will go in unto the altar of God
To God, Who giveth joy to my youth.

PENSAMIENTOS
CONSUELO MARIA ALCALA

The sounds of the raindrops falling on top of the cement patio in the back yard of my home are steady and continuous. They make a soft and sad music of wind and water, moving and hitting the ground and the tree leaves. I guess this afternoon my soul feels sad. Through the bedroom window I see raindrops falling like tears rolling down my cheeks. Some of the raindrops are just there on the window, motionless, static, as if there were no time, no wind to move them, no more tears to cry. However, others keep on falling down, telling my soul that the tears are healing the very heart of the universe. A universe of memories transports me to a different time, a different moment in my life.

"Look, Sweetheart, do you like these flowers? I will plant them in the new red brick planter I just finished in front of the house." Thus spoke my father, who every spring would go to the store to buy different colorful flowers to plant around the house. This time he had selected pansies which in Spanish are called "thoughts" (*pensamientos*). The pansies were velvety, emanating incredibly rich colors. I take a petal and caress my cheeks and pass it over my lips. I feel the smooth, delicate and soothing texture. He had bought different colored pansies: purple, yellow,

hot pink, and white ones. The petals had different blends of
colors and shades that gave the flowers a majestic and splendid
look. He was excited like a child and wanted to share with me
the beauty of such lovely gifts. He also wanted the approval that
his choice was correct. I could not appreciate the pleasure he
derived from the flowers then, but I went along with him and
expressed his same gusto. Every morning he would sweep the
big yard, and whenever he had time, he would work around
the house and garden, upgrading them. He wanted to make the
house look gay, full of light, and beautiful. His house, the best in
the neighborhood, was his pride. The work he put into it gave
him a lot of satisfaction.

It has been ten years since he passed away, and when it rains
my heart feels the pain of the separation—the pain of not
sharing any more moments with him: all those escaping
moments that I wish I had shared, and never did. I wish I could
have opened sooner to the understanding of the beauty of
nature, to be able to appreciate his love for it. I see the fuschia,
orange, pink, and white bouganvilleas on top of the back fence
of my patio that have reached the roof of the patio shade
and fall across it like cascades of a million colors. I see that this
flowing cascade of flowers is the nest for many birds that come
and go. I close my eyes and transport myself to the sun bed of
flowers—I feel their rich colors spreading all over my body.
I remember pictures my father took of me in the back yard of
our old house next to the eucalyptus tree, which was surrounded
by fuschia bougainvilleas. He was a proud father who cherished

PENSAMIENTOS (CONT.)

his children. Every time I look at the nourishing bougainvilleas in my back yard, I remember my father's quiet love for his children. I know that father loved us; he loved us very much and suffered with us all the moments of our pain.

Every year, I find myself going to the store at the beginning of spring to buy *pensamientos* (thoughts). Each one of the pansies represents a message of love from my father. I have a genuine appreciation for flowers. I feel they are a colorful part of the many gifts that God has given to humanity to remind us that He loves us very much, and that beauty is all around us—at our reach. We just have to look at nature with our heart to be able to see God's beauty everywhere.

As I am writing about God's gifts, I look through the window and see a very small bird looking toward me as it sits on a branch of the fuschia bougainvilleas. The bird stretches its wings, looks all around, and starts chirping. The rain is no longer falling, the skies are clear and the colors of the wet trees, flowers, and houses look richer and brighter, creating a colorful contrast with the blue sky. The tree leaves look greener and glossy, with raindrops shining leaves, sparkling like morning dew. All the surroundings look very calm and quiet. On the horizon, I can see the heavenly light through the last clouds in the West. I feel God's presence surrounding us all. "Father," I whispered, looking at the little bird, "I love you very much too," and I close my eyes to be in touch with the heavenly light. When I open my eyes and look at the branch where the little bird was sitting, I see that the bird is gone. However, I feel an immense tranquility in my heart.

"Father, " I say, "I see the rainbow coming out in the sky. Yes, Father, it is the same rainbow you saw when I rushed you to the hospital that endless, anxious afternoon. It was one of God's last gifts you saw before you lost your sight momentarily, and before you entered that huge, concrete hospital from which you never came out again. Yes, Father, I see the colors in the sky. I see the rainbow, and I feel your spirit."

I open my eyes and look through the window and to my surprise, I see that the little bird is back, sitting on the branch of my bougainvillea a second time. I look at it, without moving a muscle. As the bird again takes flight, I notice it starts flapping its wings rapidly. I get up from my chair to look closer and see its long beak. "It's a hummingbird, Father! It's a hummingbird!" My own special symbol of God's presence. Over the years I called this tiny and lovely bird my own God's messenger. My prayers have been answered, my thoughts of love have been conveyed to my father's spirit, my eyes are filled with tears of joy. It's no longer raining. Thank you, God!

Defining My Curiosities
Carmen Solis

How do I define Life?
How do I define being a Chicana?
How do I define love?
How do I define virginity?

So many questions and not enough answers.
My parents told me that being a *señorita* means being pure,
walking through *altar vestida de blanco*.

But living in this world where everyone lives different from my *cultura*
makes me question my morals.

I have learned that love is respect,

Communication,
   Knowledge,
      Trust.

To love you is to respect you *en las buenas y en las malas*.
To love you is to trust you, not necessarily to understand
everything you say but to try to understand.
To love you is to think of you and feel my heart pound like crazy.

To love you is to have those nonsense, crazy conversations.
To love you is to support you in everything you do.
To love you is to miss you.
To love you is to walk with you,

Fly with you,
   Dream with you.

But you tell me that if I love you, I must give my *pureza*.

Is that how you define love?
Is that how everyone defines love?

If you define love as sex,
Then tell me what is to make love?

No,

Having sex is not making love.

To make love is not only *entregarte a la persona que amas,*
Making love is understanding that once your body and my body
become one we are going to be together forever,
And ever,
    And ever,
        Para siempre

To make love is to feel warm bodies becoming one, and to feel our
sweet lips caressing each other.
To make love is to give our heart and soul.
To make love is to become one *con la bendición de Dios.*

I close my eyes and I feel my tears rolling down my cheeks as I think,

How do I show you that I love you?
If my definition of love is not sex and having sex is not making love

I know that I love you because when I'm with you *mi corazón palpita
como loco* and my whole body is filled with
a wonderful sensation that I can't explain.

I know that I love you because as the time passes by, we decide
to be together forever, and become one *con la bendición de Dios.*

I am willing to show you that I love you.

But for right now I can only tell you that I know I love you because
when my innocent lips tenderly caress your lips, I give you my heart
and soul as I slowly whisper

I Love You,

    I Love You,

        Te Amo.

A Plea for Love

José Jaimes

Too often I ask myself:
Who is she?
Where is she?

The love of my life for which I'm
longing;
Could it be that I was meant to be
alone?
So much I've searched,
So much it hurts,
So much the pain,
I'm losing faith.

Too often I ask myself,
Is it I?
I'd give my life for a friend,
I'd give my life to eternal love.

A broken heart,
Why even remember.
As much as I try,
It is just not enough.

I give,
Not expecting anything in return.
I give because it feels good.
I give because I choose to.
Though If I earn something in return
Love is what I ask for.

Who is it I secretly love this time?
Who am I thinking of as I write this?
That only my frightened heart knows
Frightened to make the first move,
Frightened to be rejected.

Every one needs someone,
And to wish doesn't hurt,
Or does it?

Woman Mica Valdez

LA RAZA
LA RAZA CLUB OF VISTA HIGH SCHOOL

Cuando somos niños, no nos damos cuenta
De quien esta a nuestro lado, solo queremos jugar
Compartir juguetes y tener amigos.

Cuando crecemos nos damos cuenta del
Color de la gente, de que si tienen los ojos
Rasgados, si son ricos o pobres, si son blancos o
Morenos. ¿Por qué?

¿Por qué no podemos ser como eramos
Antes? Sin darnos cuenta de esas cosas tan
Significantes. Dios nos hizo a todos iguales, todos
Somos humanos en esta vida. Solo hay una raza,
"La raza humana."

¿Por qué ahora nos importa y ponemos nombre
Unos a otros. Si ves a dos niños jugando, no los
Verás diciendose nombres ofencivos, pero si ves a
Dos personas mayores platicando loderas. Es el
Racismo tan cruel y despiadado.

En los papeles importantes te pregunta ¿qué
Raza eres? Eres Hispano, Anglo-sajon, o
Afro-Americano? Tantos nombres que te ponen.
Te ponen un título. ¿Por qué los humanos somos
Asi, si todos somos y siempre seremos una raza?

"La raza humana."

Death Mica Valdez

Lauren Jennifer Ferrer

El Amor
de Juan Sandoval
Lisette Ordorica

It was a sleepy summer day in the pueblito of Jalpa, Zacatecas.
On the ranches on the outskirts of the city, the cows peacefully
chewed their cud, while chickens squabbled in their coop. On
the ranch of Tepesala, Señora Pedroza bustled about her kitchen,
preparing *cena* for her six daughters. It would be a simple
meal, since her husband and sons were away from the ranch on
business. Her two oldest daughters, Evangelina and Consuelo,
helped her. Now the reason I tell you this is because these
two ladies were quite popular in the small ranch community.
Last year, Consuelo had won the title of harvest beauty queen,
and her five sisters were no disappointment to the eyes, either.
Many a hopeful fellow had approached the porch of the Pedroza
ranch with hat in hand, hoping to be received by one of the
illustrious girls. However, very few obtained the approval of the
four Pedroza brothers, who were characteristically protective
of their sisters. The youngest, Julianita, had recently turned 16,
the age at which she would be allowed to date. Señora Pedroza
and her husband, Federico, ruled their daughters with a strict
but loving hand. Days of working in the sun in the cornfields,
or pounding wet clothes against a rock had not marred the
complexion or good humor of any of the daughters. Although
their arms were strong and healthy from churning butter and
milking cows, they were every inch ladies.

EL AMOR DE JUAN SANDOVAL (CONT.)

The loveliness of Julianita did not escape the attention of many of the town's men, young or old. It especially did not escape the eyes of Juan Sandoval, a neighbor of the Pedrozas. But much to his chagrin, Julianita had taken up with a boy closer to her own age, Ismael Medina. She had always been cordial to Juan whenever he came to speak with Don Pedroza about town matters, but he now realized that this was not enough. At 25, he had yet to marry, or even find any prospects. He suddenly realized that he loved Julianita truly, madly, and deeply. (I should note that he came to this conclusion while nursing his umpteenth Dos Equis Cerveza in Chato's Cantina.) Staring into the bar mirror across from him, he conjured up an image of her sweet face, framed by the schoolgirl pigtails that she still sported. She seemed to radiate light as she smiled at him, and only him, and the image was so beautiful that it brought tears to his eyes.

"S-shato," he slurred as he pointed to the mirror, "Shato, at's the gurl I'm gonna marry!"

Chato followed his finger to Juan's own image in the mirror, and nodded his head, playing along. "Oh yeah, Juan, she's real pretty. You're a lucky guy!"

Juan smiled and nodded his head in agreement until his eyes narrowed in suspicion. "Hey, you're not gonna tryn' take her from me, are you? 'Cause she's MINE, you hear, and if I can't have her, no one can!" His frown deepened as the radiant image of Julianita suddenly acquired a veil, and then, to his horror, Ismael appeared on her arm. He suddenly realized how great a threat lay between him and his angel. Well, there was no way he would let any snooty Medina get in the way of his destiny. Julianita really loved Juan, he knew it in his heart…he only needed to make her realize it. Yet he knew that Don Pedroza would never let him past his threshold.

This was not a problem. In the false bravado that comes with drunkenness, he devised a plan. All he would need to do is catch her at dusk while she was doing some chores outside by herself, come by on his horse and literally sweep her off her feet. He couldn't get in trouble for kidnapping if they got married, he reasoned. And once she saw the lengths he went to for her love, she would want to marry him instantly, right?

After supper, Doña Pedroza sent her daughters out to the corral to pick some of the ripe fruit off of the papaya trees. Doña Pedroza was sitting in the front room, making the best of the fading light as she mended a pair of stockings. Her head raised inquisitively as she heard a horse thunder into the yard. It was not the friendly trot of a neighbor coming to visit, and she was worried. Peeking out of the front windows, she saw that it was Juan Sandoval. "What does he want?" she thought irritably. With the Señor and her sons in Aguascalientes, she was in no mood to deal with suitors. She decided that she would briskly send him on his way. She jumped in surprise when instead of the polite knock that she expected, Juan burst through the door that was never kept locked.

"What in the world do you think you're doing?" she demanded of him.

Juan, suddenly realizing where he was, was struck with embarrassment as he faced the stern woman.

"I, uh, I…I'm gonna marry Juliana." He muttered.

EL AMOR DE JUAN SANDOVAL (CONT.)

"Oh, are you now?" replied Doña Pedroza. "What makes you think she'll have you? And even if she did, what makes you think we'd let her?"

This only angered Juan, and his embarrassment dissipated, turning into anger. In another burst of bravado, he drew close to the petite woman's face.

"Oh, she'll have me alright! She'll have me because I'm going to take her! You'll see, you'll see how happy she is when I come on my horse to take her away!" In his anger, he did not realize that he had drawn his pistola and was waving it around in the air. "You'll be sorry, you'll all be sorry!" And with this he departed, slamming the door behind him.

Señora Pedroza was left in shock, trembling from head to foot. She had never dealt with anything like this before. It was the only time in her life that she thought having beautiful daughters was possibly a curse instead of a blessing. Well, there was only one thing to do, she thought. Juliana needed to be hidden away immediately. If not, she would surely be kidnapped. She remembered the shotgun her husband always kept under the bed. That would have to do, for it was too late now to send one of the girls for help. She ran out to the back and called for the girls to come in.

"Ay, Julianita, Julianita!" her mother said. "Who have you been batting your eyelashes at now?"

"What do you mean, *madrecita*?" replied Juliana. "You know that Ismael and I are novios!"

"Yes, I know, and so does Juan Sandoval. He just came and told me that he was planning to kidnap you. We must hide you away!"

"WHAT!" gasped all six sisters.

And the next thing that Julianita knew, she was locked in the barn with a shotgun and an admonition by her mother to shoot if Juan even attempted to get in. She passed a long, sleepless, and uneventful night in the barn. Although she was somewhat afraid, she was also somewhat smug. How many other girls had men taking such risks for them? She knew that it wasn't many. She smiled to herself as she leaned back in the hay, knowing that by morning the story would be all over town. What a reputation of a heartbreaker she would have!

After she was found safe in the morning, her mother promptly sent her to live with her *tía* for the remaining two weeks until her brothers came back. And as for Juan, he woke up in his front yard the next morning with a dim recollection of what had happened. He was so ashamed at his behavior that he felt he should go apologize to the family at once. However, he was warned by the townspeople that all four Pedroza brothers had instructions to shoot him promptly if he was ever seen even near the Pedroza ranch. He then knew that no family in Jalpa in their right mind would ever let him near their daughter. He thought it best to leave town until he could make a respectable name for himself, and was never seen again.

As for Juliana, things never quite worked out with Ismael, especially when an older boy named Raul Ordorica came to live in town. When he met Juliana, he dropped his current girlfriend, my mother dropped Ismael, and they were married several months later. They lived a happy life in the United States and have six lovely children. But not too lovely, for the youngest daughter has yet to be threatened with kidnapping.

ME

ORLANDO MALFAVON

He sits and stares
Never blinking
And he never feels anything
But pain
He sits
With the emotions of yesterday
How could he leave this place?
How did he die?
Why wasn't it me?
That is what he thinks
And why does it have to happen
Like this especially when he
Is me.

Photographs by Jennifer Ferrer

North of the Border
Marisol Truax

North of the border, so they say,
There's lots of food, and plenty of play.

There's plenty of Chicanos there already.
The life up there is plenty heady.

The streets are mostly paved with gold
And nobody there ever gets old.

All of the houses are made of wood.
And can withstand the wettest flood.

No more hunger, no more grief.
There's luxury beyond belief.

Everybody has a credit card,
And the work to be done is not very hard.

Good bye, Mama. Goodbye, Dad
I'm sure my leaving won't make you sad.

One less hungry mouth to feed.
And an acre less of land to weed.

I'll miss you both, and you'll miss me,
But when I'm gone you'll shout with glee.

You raised me till I was fit to travel.
So now I've got to hit the gravel.

I'll come back someday, or send for you
And all my brothers and sisters too.

'Cause north of the border, all is swell,
While back down here, the life is hell.

I know a new day may be aborning.
Mexico may have a great good morning.

Honest people may be taking over,
And all the poor may live in clover.

And if they do, I will come back,
Join you and Mom across the track.

But if that never does take place,
I'll send for you and the whole darned race.

So farewell, farewell my Guadalajara
Perhaps I'll be back day after tomorrow.

WHO WOULD'VE THOUGHT
JOSÉ JAIMES

Who would've thought, that a simple stare,
Would mark the beginning of what we have today.
Your rounded cheeks, your honey eyes,
The whiteness of your soul,
The redness of your heart,
A reality hard to find.

Who would've thought, that destiny would choose us,
It took its time though, but we are finally here.
For years we've known each other,
Though I'm glad that's what it took.
For the best relationships begin as good friends,
Later transforming to passionate love.

With an open heart I write this,
For to love is hard to admit.
Though let pride take a rest,
And let out what my true feelings seek:

Basically, that one person who will stay when everyone leaves;
That one person who will love me and never let go;
That one person who will share with me her darkest secrets
and deepest fantasies;

Surrendering to me in body and soul;
Finally that one person for whom I will be their everything,
and who will fight maturely
For me when a third person wants to come in,
and who will never give up until
We are buried together only to fall in love again in the next life.

It is early to tell if you are the one, but let destiny take its course,
Though who would've thought.

Before my pride comes back,
Let me confess that I love you, and that you fulfill me.
I just hope that you feel the same for me.

At last, who would've thought,
That a simple stare would mark the beginning,
Up to the point,
That I would finally let out those three difficult words:

I…Love…You

THE DARKNESS
RICARDO MENDOZA

"Who's there?"

"Me."

"Me, who?"

"Me!"

"Don't get smart. You want me to turn you off?"

"Go ahead, if you can."

"All right. Who are you?"

"Ricardo."

"You're a pitiful excuse…I'm going to send you back to grammar school."

"That's the name I was given."

"Then I don't know you!"

"So what?"

"What do you want here?"

"I'm thinking."

"Thinking about what?"

"About all the shit. All the bologna. All this bloody mess wrapped up in skin."

"You're too uptight."

"It's too tight in here. Too many possibilities."

"Pick a dot."

"What do you mean?"

"Pick a dot and follow it."

"I don't see anything—I don't have eyes."

"Pick a dot."

"What the hell for? It's all shit anyway."

"What about your schoolwork?"

"You mean the warrior-king bit?"

"Yes."

"Bull. Nothing but bull."

"Years of studying."

"Marking time, that's all. Just marking time."

"There's no such thing."

"I don't have eyes."

"Time exists only when movement exists. It's a sensation you get when you think."

(echo) "What?—What?"

"Space exists! There is no space. Fill the spaces!"

"I'm crying."

THE DARKNESS (CONT.)

"You're always crying. Fill the spaces!"

"All right, but just remember that I'm no Mexican."

"What's that supposed to mean?"

"I'm no Mexican. Just that. Make what you want out of it."

"You know, you're starting to sound just like all the other idiot children."

"I don't care. Just remember! I'm no Mexican!"

Sano and Corvera arrived in El Toro around midnight. They exited the I-5 at the giant bronzed globe and took a right on River's Edge Highway, drove north about five miles, then turned left into a dirt driveway leading to the farmhouse and the old wooden shack. Corvera got out of the car and knocked three times on the plastic door. No one answered. He knocked again.

"I guess all the guys must be asleep," Corvera told Sano. "Either that, or they don't want to open the door." Sometimes as many as twelve guys slept in the shack.

Corvera parked the old Gremlin under a tree, and Sano pulled the sleeping bags from the cargo area.

"What the hell?" Sano said. "I've slept in worse places than this lots of times. Besides, I'm in the best of company. *Verdad, compadre?*"

Sano pulled down the window on the passenger side of the car and felt the warm breeze on his face. He smelled the corn stalks but couldn't see a thing. Outside it was totally black. The moon was hiding behind the thickest fog Sano had ever seen. It was because of that same fog that it had taken them so long to drive up from Otay. Sano put his hand up to his face, trying to see how dark it was, but no matter how close he held his hand to his eyes, he couldn't see it. Finally, the tip of his right index finger poked him in the left eye and he gave up.

"That must be what a blind man sees," Sano thought to himself, and he remembered Kim Brown, the blind kid from Roosevelt Junior High. Sano had seen him sitting next to the main gate, and he had been curious about the still, quiet boy. Then he had seen the dark shadows around the boy's deep, sunken eyes and had realized that the boy was blind.

"Who's there?"

"Hi! My name is Sano. How you doing?" He said it as best as his English would allow, but he knew that his Yaqui-Spanish was getting in the way.

"Who?"

"Sano. My name is Sano. Sano Santander."

"I don't know you."

"No, you don't know me. I just wanted to come over and talk to you."

"Why?"

"No reason. I was just on my way home and I saw you sitting here, so I said to myself, 'why not go over and talk to him.' "

"What about?"

"Nothing. You know, just shoot the shit."

THE DARKNESS (CONT.)

"Are you Mexican?"

"No."

"What are you? You sound Spanish."

"I'm a Yaqui."

"Yaqui? What's that?"

"An Indian. I'm from Arizona."

"Mexican Indian?"

"On both sides."

"What do you mean?"

"Yaquis run on both sides of the border."

"So, what are you doing around here?"

"Here? You mean here, sitting next to you?"

"No. Here in the school."

"Me?"

"Yes."

"I go to school here. Just like you."

"Oh."

And Kim didn't say anything else after that, so Sano got embarrassed and left. He realized later that blind men were not always looking for a conversation. He left, thinking, "My name's not Sano anyway—even if that is what I told Corvera."

Corvera and Sano took turns going to the outhouse. There was only one flashlight, and they were not about to sit down on a toilet seat without knowing what they were sitting on.

"Some guy got bit by a scorpion," Corvera told Sano. "Served him right."

Afterwards, they ate the last two burritos and settled down for the night. Corvera would sleep in the driver's seat and Sano in the back. Sano saw Corvera jump inside his sleeping bag, but he thought the night was too warm for sleeping bags, so he rolled his sleeping bag into a ball and used it for a pillow.

"Fucking Corvera," he was to say later, "you should've told me how cold it got around here."

Corvera only laughed. He would have warned him, but Chuparosa had taught him to teach others by example. Besides, he'd really gotten a good laugh out of it.

"*Wakan-tan-kahe eh ixstish eneand*," he had said. "I set the example. If you don't want to follow it, that's your concern."

Usually, Corvera slept in the dirty shack with all the other farm workers, so it was all the same to him. He was used to the cold, to the hard tortillas, used to the cold, gritty coffee.

"Hell, when the field truck arrrives to pick everybody up, there's hardly time to wash and get dressed," he'd told Sano. "You finish dressing on the way to the fields—the truck is going down the highway at ninety miles per hour—you're trying to hold on to your hat, and the truck comes to a skidding stop at the irrigation ditches. Then everybody gets out. In the morning, it's all one mad hurry."

THE DARKNESS (CONT.)

Corvera was the only brown face on the melons. The other Mexicans worked the corn.

"Four o'clock in the morning, and everything is icy cold. They run the water in the ditches all night long. You're still half asleep. You come by and stumble into them and get your feet all muddy, then you spend the rest of the day walking around in shoes that feel like cement. The cold doesn't stop at your feet, either. It just goes up your legs, into your bones and stays there. Five, five-thirty, and your bones start hurting."

Sano woke up at two in the morning struggling to get into his sleeping bag. As soon as he had warmed up a bit, he went back to his dreams. He had only an hour left, and he dreamed about his girlfriend, Yanda, and the first time they had made love. The day he'd lost his virginity. He was laughing in his sleep.

Sano was standing in a sea of grass, feeling the wind at his face and listening to the screaming of each individual blade. The shine on his face testified to the presence of the sun, but he could not find it, much as he tried. Everything was tall grass and blue sky. The air smelled of mint and chamomile, though there was none to be seen. He felt an urge to walk, and soon he came upon a single mound of barren earth that stuck out five, ten feet above the tall grass. It was a lonely spot with few rocks in a sea of grass, and the wind was pushing him on. It took him five minutes to climb the mound. He wanted to have a look beyond the meadow, but it wasn't easy; the wind kept pushing him off balance. He almost fell several times. But the wind seemed to be protecting him too, pulling him up the mound. When he got to the top, he looked in every direction but saw nothing but grass. Toward the east, something was calling him. There the sky seemed somehow lighter, and he thought that he could see a faint suggestion of mountains, or perhaps of concrete, just faint whispers of forms.

The wind changed directions and grew stronger. It seemed alive, intelligent. At first Sano was afraid, but soon the wind took hold of his heart and rushed through him to the very depths of his soul. He surrendered his will to the force of the wind, and the wind lifted him off the mound. He was ascending into the heavens—higher and higher—until he was just shy of the first clouds. There the wind held him in check. He was amazed at the reality of flight and at the maneuverings of the wind. It never occurred to him that it was unnatural.

"God wants me to fly," he kept saying to himself. "That's why I'm having this dream."

Finally, far beyond the meadow, Sano saw a line of eucalyptus trees that formed an unfathomable wall. He wanted to climb even higher to see, but the savage sound of the wind scared him, and he began to shake violently. He was losing his balance. He fell backwards over himself, fell down to the earth as rapidly as his thoughts. As he approached the earth, he was ready for the hard blow, but instead he landed on the soft grass and cried himself to sleep.

Corvera woke up at four-thirty and wasn't surprised to find Sano fully awake.

"You should have told me how cold it got around here," he said, but Corvera only smiled.

They got up and washed. Then they drove the Gremlin to the

THE DARKNESS (CONT.)

melon field and asked the owner, Santini, for a job for Sano.

"He's too scrawny," Santini told Corvera. "He won't be able to handle the sun. He can work the corn if he wants to, but he's too scrawny for the melons."

Santini didn't speak directly to Sano. "'Cause that's the way you do things in the fields," Corvera had warned Sano. "You speak to the boss when you're spoken to." So it was no surprise to Sano that Santini treated him like dirt.

"Give him a chance, boss," Corvera insisted. "He's strong."

Corvera wanted someone to shoot the shit with. All the other guys on the melon crews were Anglos, and they didn't speak his language. They were from that watch-ya-ma-call-it-town, the town near El Toro. They considered themselves the cream of the watermelon crop. Their parents owned most of the farms around the valley, so most of them had been picking watermelons ever since their junior years.

"Look, Corvera, remember those Mexicans I hired the other day? Well, they just couldn't hack it. Mexicans don't do well on the melons. They pass out before they've hardly started. Hell, I even had to take one guy to the hospital all the way in Santa Ana. I wasted two hours doing that. Then when I came back, the two other Mexicans passed out too. The whole day was a sorry waste of time. I'm telling you, Corvera, I ain't gonna be repeating that today. I don't know what it is about you Mexicans—you just don't seem to be able to handle it."

"You know I'm a hard worker, boss."

"Well, sure, Corvera. I don't mean nothing against you. You're different. I mean you're a hard worker, I know that. You handle the melons real good, too. It's just that that—well—most Mexicans don't seem to be able to lift those big melons, you know. Too undernourished, I guess."

"Boss, I promise you, this guy can do the work. Watch this. Make a muscle Sano. Make a muscle! See that, boss? See that? He's got a lot of muscle." Santini started laughing.

"All right, Corvera. All right. You win. But if he goes down on the job, I'll hold you responsible. I'm not going to waste another day driving around the whole goddamned county for no stupid Mexicans. If he goes down, you deal with it."

"Sure, boss. Thank you, boss. You won't regret it. He's got a lot of muscle. You'll see."

"All right. All right. You put him on the fourth row and show him the ropes. If he can't handle that, well, then he's out."

Santini turned away and clapped his hands. "All right, let's get going. Everybody up! Get to it!"

By the time five o'clock arrived, a slow steady rhythm of work rose up from the field. Melons flew under the light of the white, foggy moon. On the I-5, millions of cars hummed silently past the melon field, yet no one paid much attention.

"Civilized technology."

"What?"

"Civilized technology. Cars! Society's mechanized blood!"

"What?"

THE DARKNESS (CONT.)

"Like in the story, Goddamn it. Weren't you listening?"

"Well, no, not really. Not with my mind, anyway."

"What do you mean, 'not with my mind.' With what, then?"

"With the sensations. I liked the bit about the river of ideals and morals."

"What do you mean? We haven't gotten to that part yet."

"I also liked the part about the cars being society's blood, spilling all over the place."

"No one said anything about cars being blood."

"Well, not yet. I'm going ahead of the silences. We'll get there, don't worry."

"What are you talking about? I'm not going anywhere."

"Oh, yes you are. Much as you try, you're only a man."

"I'm no fucking man!"

"What are you, then?"

"I'm more."

"More like what?"

"I'm just more, that's all. What the hell do you care, anyway?"

"You're the one that cares."

"All I know is that I'm more."

"More than what?"

"More than a Mexican."

"Back to that, again?"

"I'm no Mexican!"

"All right, so you're not a Mexican. Then what are you?"

"I'm a song."

"Now you've said something!"

"I'm a song in a mist—I'm a floating mist—vibrating through a pitch whose name I know."

"Now you're saying something!"

"   ."

"Now you know."

"   ."

"Hey!"

"   ."

"Hey!"

"   ."

"You still there?"

"   ."

"Hey!"

"They had nothing to barter."

"What?"

THE DARKNESS (CONT.)

"Compared to the rhythm of the dirt and sky, the motorists were sluggish ghosts, moving through a field of watermelons."

The melon patch ran along both sides of the freeway for a stretch of five miles. It was wide enough to touch the Santa Anna creek on the east side and long enough to crisscross the oceanic bluffs on the west. Each watermelon row ran down to an infinite point on the horizon. Each man picked and tossed his own melons, and he caught the melons coming at him from his right. One guy was on the tractor, and one guy rode the trailer. The man closest to the trailer had the hardest job because he had to catch all of the melons, as well as toss them up to the trailer. That took a lot of strength. Sano was on the fourth row; he had the easiest job. All he had to do was toss his melons over to Corvera. He didn't have to catch anyone's melons—that took extra energy.

"Don't bend your back, bend your knees," Corvera told him. "If you start bending your back, you won't last an hour."

Six o'clock came, and Sano was tossing them like a pro. Melons large and small were quickly being dispensed of. But Sano didn't know the tricks of the trade, and he squandered too much energy moving back and forth.

"Don't run around so much. Take it easy. You're gonna run down your batteries before the day's over."

By seven o'clock, the sun was showing its ugly red face, and Sano started moving more slowly. He took off his shirt and started tearing out the hearts of the watermelons.

"Don't eat so many melons, either. You'll get stuffed. We still got a long way to go before the noon break."

The sun passed nine o'clock, and Sano started weaving. The muscles in his legs started to quiver and tremble, and he started getting stiff all around his chest and arms. At nine-thirty, Sano stopped bending his knees and started bending at the waist, using his back for the lift. Corvera knew he had to do something or Sano was going to run out of juice, fast. He put him on the third row and started handing him the melons, walking them over to him.

Eleven o'clock and Sano's arms became totally useless. He was holding them up by sheer will. The sun was beating down on him, slapping him around. He felt like fainting, but he knew that Corvera was depending on him, so he held on.

"Hold on, Sano. All you've got to do is hold on one more hour. Then you can rest."

Sano heard Corvera talking to him, but his mind was far away, on a green meadow. He was profoundly tired. He started to fall asleep, right there on his feet. Someone was shaking him.

"Come on, Sano, hold on! You can do it! Don't give up on me. I know you can do it. C'mon. Just one more hour."

Sano heard Corvera talking to him, but he didn't believe in himself anymore. He stayed on his feet though.

Sano said, "I can't do it, Corvera. I'm done in. Really. I've got to quit." But he knew he wouldn't quit.

"Stay on your feet," Corvera told him. "Just stay on your feet."

Corvera was now doing the work for both of them. Sano opened his eyes and saw that the other guys on the crew were also helping him. Even the tractor had slowed down to keep pace with him. Everyone wanted him to make it, Sano realized. Then Santini was standing next to him, watching him.

"He's going to fire me now," Sano thought. "I've really blown it for Corvera."

As Sano closed his eyes he knew he was letting his best friend down…

He was standing on the same mound of barren earth. At the same place, in the middle of the same valley. He felt the lift of the wind, and he ascended to the line of scattered clouds. But he couldn't see beyond the line of eucalyptus trees, so he went higher, above the clouds, above the calling birds. This time he felt sure. He wasn't afraid. Far beyond, he saw the valley of the city with its many trees. He passed over the trees and out of the green meadow. As he approached the heart of the city, the day turned to night and he descended into a wide street lined with scores of rubber trees. He flew down the middle of the street, ten feet above the asphalt. The street seemed familiar, and he soon realized that it was the street where he used to play with his friends. He touched the surface of the asphalt with his rubber-soled shoes and left streaks on the pavement. The drag slowed him down, and he was walking among the sounds of barking dogs. He turned the corner and saw the house that he was born in. He was home.

"Snap out of it!" someone's voice said.

"What's going on?"

"He's okay." He heard Santini's voice.

Sano was now in the back of an empty trailer. He looked up and saw the crew of men standing all around him, most of them laughing. The tractor wasn't moving.

"Lunch time!" he heard Santini say. "Lunch time!"

Corvera was sitting next to him. The laughter sounded in his ears.

"It's lunch time," said Corvera, brandishing a big, wide smile. "You made it! Let's eat."

CONTRIBUTOR BIOGRAPHIES

CONSUELO MARIA ALCALA   44

Born in San Diego in 1951, she worked with young children
as a bilingual preschool teacher for over ten years. In 1991,
when she published her first book of songs entitled, *Primavera,
Primavera, Nuevas Canciones y Rimas para Pequeños*, she had
been diagnosed with chronic lymphocytic leukemia. While she
battled the disease going through chemotherapy, she continued
working eight hours, went to night school, and continued with
her writings for her following books. Her efforts in producing
beautiful and enjoyable songs for children and their teachers on
themes for all the seasons became her most important goal.
She published a second book and cassette of songs for summer:
*El Verano Vestido de Sol y De Color, Nuevas Canciones en
Español Para Pequeños*. Her third book and cassette is a
collection of fun songs in Spanish to use during fall. The title is:
*El Otoño Ya Llegó y La Señora Ardillon, Mas Nuevas Canciones
en Español Para Pequeños*. Consuelo Maria used to say that
writing the songs gave her a lot of joy because she vividly
could imagine the children having fun with her songs, and
that brought her immeasurable satisfaction. She also kept
the teacher in mind in her writings. Her books were adopted
by various school districts in the San Diego County area.

CONTRIBUTORS (CONT.)

She felt that songs in Spanish are needed for many themes and concepts, and to encourage children to love their language and culture. The songs express a special love and appreciation of nature, family, and that children are the most important, delicate, and unique part of nature. Songs, she believed, have to be written in a way that motivate children to participate actively during music and movement activities inside the classroom and outside in the yard.

Consuelo Maria's goal of producing a beautiful collection of songs to leave as a contribution for young children and their teachers was fulfilled. She lost her battle in October of 1998.

LINDA AMADOR   20

Born and raised in San Diego County, she received her BA in Art at Cal State University, San Marcos (CSUSM). She is in a Master's program at CSUSM. Her art medium is graphite and assemblage art, and she has presented her art throughout California. Amador began her academic career as an adult learner attending Palomar Community College.

JOEY AZUL   15

Joey Azul grew up on a small farm in Wisconsin with five brothers and sisters. She received her BA in Sociology from the University of California, San Diego. As a student she participated in campus activist politics. She also earned a Master's Degree at San Diego State University. Joey is now preparing for a degree in art at Palomar and plans to transfer to a graduate program in Art.

ARI CASTELLANOS 36

Ari is a former Palomar student in Chicano Studies.

JENNIFER FERRER 54, 61

Born in Humacao, Puerto Rico, January 12, 1984. Moved
to California in 1998 and started school in Center City High
School. While she was in high school she started at Palomar
College and finished high school at the age of 16. While in
college she took several classes of photography, and three years
later she was accepted at The Art Institute of California–LA
to continue on her major Video Production before she went on
to create the video and production company, Ferrer Productions.

MAINARDO (MIKE) FLORES 37

Born in Mexico City and raised in Escondido, he is currently
working on a photography book based on Latino culture.
He writes poetry and short stories from his cultural perspective.

SHERRIE GONZALES-KOLB 3, 6, 11

An undergraduate in I/O psychology program, she is a poet
and a writer, published in literature magazines, such as Palomar
College's *Bravura*, CSUSM's *PLS*, *The Chiron Review*, and
HazMat Review. She served as host for Southwestern College's
Poetry Slam in recognition of Women's History Month.
Her lifelong dream is to teach underrepresented populations,
so that they might find emotional health to strive toward upward
mobility and life satisfaction. She also writes two poetry blogs:

www.icewomancometh.blogspot.com/
www.timeout4now.blogspot.com/

CONTRIBUTORS (CONT.)

JOSÉ JAIMES   18, 50, 64

José was born in Mexico City, Mexico and was a member and
president of MEChA at Palomar College. He earned a BA from
Cal State University, San Marcos in Psychology with a minor in
Visual and Performing Arts. He plans to teach at the high school
level. José plays competitive soccer and enjoys the arts and
is a leading member of the dance group Amigos by Legacy in
Vista. José loves to write and enjoys school and is motivated
to write a book in the future. He is currently director of the
dance company Tierra Caliente in Vista, California.

ORLANDO MALFAVON   60

Enrolled as a student of Palomar College in Chicano and
Chicana Literature classes, Fall 2001.

ALEX MARTINEZ   28

Alex Martinez attended San Marcos High School and began his
studies at Palomar College this summer. His major interests
are creative writing, art, and journalism. Alex aspires one day to
be a published author or art illustrator.

RICARDO MENDOZA   2, 4, 66

Ricardo Mendoza was an assistant professor of Chicana/o
Literature in the Multicultural Studies Department at Palomar
College in the early 1990's. He received his Master of Fine Arts
from San Diego University in creative writing.

LISETTE ORDORICA   55

A former Palomar College student who graduated in June 2002 from CSUSM with a bachelor's degree in Literature and Writing. Lisette plans to teach American Literature at the college level. She enjoys reading, and spending time with family and friends. She is completing a doctoral degree in Literature at the University of California, Riverside.

LA RAZA CLUB (VISTA HIGH SCHOOL)   52

Members from the student leaders La Raza Club in Vista, California.

YASHUHIRO SAHARA   35

Yashuhiro Sahara comes from Hamamatsu City, Japan. He came to study in the United States in 1999, majoring in recreation. He plans to develop studies in international business and one day begin an import and export business. He enjoys the ocean, surfing, and girls.

ERNESTO SANCHEZ   38

Ernesto was born in Michoacan, Mexico. His major at Palomar College is Psychology and his minor is History. His main interests are sports: basketball and boxing. He plans to become a high school counselor.

CARMEN SOLIS   48

Carmen Solis was born in LaBarca, Jalisco, Mexico and came to live in Encinitas when she was eight years old. She enjoys writing, dancing, acting, and working with children and in the future is considering teaching as a career.

CONTRIBUTORS (CONT.)

MARISOL TRUAX   62

Enrolled as a student of Palomar College in Chicano and
Chicana Literature classes, Fall 2001.

JOHN EDUARDO VALDEZ   1, 40

Born in Lemon Grove, California, he eventually graduated from
University of San Diego, majoring in philosophy and history.
He attended UC San Diego as a doctoral candidate in literature
before coming to Palomar College in 1972, where he has taught
Chicano Studies, and has served as a MEChA advisor, and Chair
of the Multicultural Studies Department.

A member of the Oxford Roundtable, he has presented papers
on Multiculturalism in America and American Foreign Policy,
the oral history of the Mexican American community from
the Mexican Revolution to World War II in Lemon Grove,
California, and Cesar Chavez' life and his fight for social
justice. Professor Valdez is developing a documentary on the
first successful desegregation court case won in March, 1931
in Lemon Grove, California.

MICA VALDEZ   10, 14, 39, 51, 53

Mica Valdez's poems, stories and artwork have appeared in
Red Ink Magazine, Kweli Journal, Mujeres de Maiz (Women
of Corn), and anthologized in *Other Tongues: Mixed-Race
Women Speak Out.* She edited *Turtle Island to Abya Yala,* a
love anthology featuring art and poetry by over sixty Native
American and Latina women with indigenous roots from
Canada to Brazil. Mica received her BA in American Studies
with an emphasis in Ethnic Studies from University of
California, Santa Cruz. While earning her MFA in Creative
Writing with an emphasis in Poetry at Mills College, she was
one of five artists awarded an American Indian Artists
Residency to work on her poetry manuscript at the Montana
Artists Refuge.

Mica Valdez is Native, mixed blood of Mexica, Swedish,
African, Irish, and Spanish descent, living in Ohlone territory
of the San Francisco Bay Area. She is a two spirit woman,
media maker and tribal scholar of pacha mama mother earth
and the great universe.

WPR BOOKS
is dedicated
to improving
portrayals and
expanding
opportunities for
Latinos in the USA

WPR BOOKS has been publishing books and directories since 1983. WPR Books has seven imprints:

Comida, Helping Hands, Heroes, Latino Insights, Latin American Insights, Para los Niños, and *Total Success.*

For more on these & other books, go to www.WPRbooks.com

The ONE BOOK every Latino & American Indian that wants to go to college or is in colleges NEEDS.

Financial resources and lots of great advice.

Includes a CD with thousands of pages of helpful information ~ and searchable scholarships.

At $30 this book & CD pays for itself immediately.

For 8th graders & up. Numerous resources at all levels from entering college to graduate school.

INCLUDES A CD WITH 3,700+ PAGES OF RESEARCH & SEARCHABLE SCHOLARSHIPS

The National Latino & American Indian Scholarship Directory

Your Source For $840+ Million To Make The College Dream Attainable

THE GUIDE TO EMPOWERING STUDENTS FOR KEY COLLEGE DECISIONS

WHY COLLEGE WILL CHANGE YOUR FUTURE
FUNDING YOUR COLLEGE DREAM
STEPS TO GOING TO COLLEGE

FINDING THE CAREER YOU WILL LOVE
POWERFUL INSIGHTS FROM 70+ LEADERS

For more on these & other books, go to www.WPRbooks.com

Calling Him Dad
The Summer My Father Appeared Out Of Nowhere
Virginia Kamhi
Award Winning Author

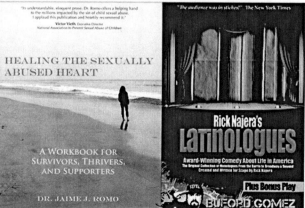

"It's understandable, eloquent prose. Dr. Romo offers a helping hand to the millions impacted by the sin of child sexual abuse. I applaud this publication and heartily recommend it."
Victor Vieth, Executive Director
National Association to Prevent Sexual Abuse of Children

HEALING THE SEXUALLY ABUSED HEART

A WORKBOOK FOR SURVIVORS, THRIVERS, AND SUPPORTERS

DR. JAIME J. ROMO

"The audience was in stitches!" The New York Times

Rick Najera's Latinologues
Award-Winning Comedy About Life in America
The Original Collection of Monologues from the Barrio to Broadway & Beyond
Created and Written for Stage by Rick Najera
Plus Bonus Play
BUFORD GOMEZ

Note from the Editors

The creative works included in this journal were submitted over a decade ago but languished before they could be brought to print due to a number of reasons. We initially thought that a small volume of these works could be printed as a fundraiser for MEChA. We are grateful to Kirk Whisler for encouraging the publication's completion in this more public form. It is a testament to the enduring legacy of these voices and stories that the material has been resurrected and released in print.

Our hope is that new stories and images will continue to be submitted for publication to showcase the beauty and the struggle that exists *en Aztlán*.

Thank you for your support.

Muchísimas gracias por su apoyo.

John Valdez
Professor of Multicultural Studies and
MEChA Advisor, Palomar College

Linda Rockafellow
Editor, The Native Tongue

CPSIA information can be obtained at www.ICGtesting.com
Printed in the USA
BVOW04s0644160614

356417BV00007B/10/P

9 781889 37933